C0-AKD-902

TOUCHING
OTHER
WORLDS

TOUCHING OTHER WORLDS

A Collection of Poems

CHRIS RAINEY

Full Court Press
Englewood Cliffs, New Jersey

First Edition

Copyright © 2011 by Chris Rainey

All rights reserved. No part of this book may be reproduced or transmitted in any form or by any means electronic or mechanical, including by photocopying, by recording, or by any information storage and retrieval system, without the express permission of the author and publisher, except where permitted by law.

Published in the United States of America
by Full Court Press, 601 Palisade Avenue
Englewood Cliffs, NJ 07632
www.fullcourtpressnj.com

ISBN 978-0-9837411-3-8
Library of Congress Control No. 2011935826

*Editing and Book Design by Barry Sheinkopf
for Bookshapers (www.bookshapers.com)*

*Cover Photo by the author
Colophon by Liz Sedlack*

DEDICATION

To Marcia,
Alyssa, Rachel, and Ava

ACKNOWLEDGMENT

A plaque near the picnic area of Flat Rock Brook Nature
Center in Englewood, New Jersey, has the following
inscription:

THIS PICNIC AREA AND 75 ACRES
OF SURROUNDING WOODLANDS IS
DEDICATED TO THE MEMORY OF

WILLIAM O. ALLISON

WHOSE FORESIGHT AND
GOODWILL PRESERVED
THIS LAND
" . . . FOR THE PURPOSE OF
PLEASING ALMIGHTY GOD
AND BENEFITTING MY
FELLOW MAN . . ."
1849–1924

I am grateful for Mr. Allison's generosity, which has en-
riched my life in profound ways as I have walked in his
woods. Many of these poems were born there.

Revelation comes to us in nature, in another person, in love, in joy, in suffering. It showers us in our childhood, when everything is viewed as miracle, as revelation. And during the better moments of our life, we know that Dostoevsky was right when he called this experience "the touching of other worlds."

—Alexander Schmemann,
Celebration of Faith: I Believe

Table of Contents

Fall

Winter

Spring

Summer

Nature

Family

Faith

Various Endings

Fall

When Vinnie Retired Two Years Ago

September used to be
a magical month for me.
School starting,
packing lunches with Snack Pack
back when the lids were steel
and the pudding was the reward
for the strength to remove
the sharp-edged tabbed tops.

Football and baseball seasons overlapped
to offer a sanctuary of sports
for those as yet to outgrow boyhood dreams.

But now no one my age still plays these games—
except one, Jamie Moyer.
Vinnie Testaverde retired two years ago.
When that happened, I retired too,
because I knew that they were all gone—
my peers—
their glory years now in the rear-view mirror.

I knew I could no longer think
that I could, if I wanted to,
step on the field again as quarterback
for the Mount Vernon High School Rams
and launch an arcing pass in the autumn air
on our first play of the game
under those Friday night lights
for a long gain as I did that night in '79

when we upset the Granite City Steelers
21 to 7.
When Vinnie left two years ago,
those thoughts of what I thought
that I could do,
if I just wanted to,
left, too.

Letting Go

(at a picnic table at Suraci Pond in Ramsey, New Jersey)

The leaves will linger a little yet
until the chilly autumn breezes push them
from their perches
and they dive down to cover nakedness below.

I walk through woods, and nature's compost
crunches underfoot
as fate forces the greens of youth to give way
to golden days before the final fateful plunge.

Beauty emerges just before leaves let go of life,
flutter and dance in grand finale to the ground
and take their place to nourish those that will remain
for next year's vernal equinox

when yet another generation
starts to falter in autumn's radiance.

First Commute

(on the occasion of my first commute into New York City)

I leave this All Saints Day in murky darkness.
Staccato steps carry me
to the bus stop.
Leaves lie fallen, victims of another autumn massacre,
the chill air signaling invading winter.
This November and December I will join the huddled
masses
entering New York.

I will depart on the dark late-autumn mornings
and step off the 166
in the dark late-autumn eventide.

Morning and evening—
the first day.

November Leaf

(riding the 166 bus from Leonia to New York)

I walked out my front door,
the wind hurrying east toward the city
while gray skies looked on,
hovering overhead as if to announce
imminent winter.

I thought again about how the screw
on the mail slot in the front door
needs repair.
It's hanging on but not secure.
Like me.

The last leaves of autumn are diving down
while others that have gone before
are getting up for one last dance
on the west wind.

I cross the street and turn to face the chill
and walk to the bus stop.
Air goes right through me,
pushes me back
like a November leaf.

There's no one at the bus stop.
I step out into the road to see past parked cars.
One other man joins me at the stop.
We do not say a word.

I am in front, and I must hail the bus.

Of all days, I must hail the bus today,
the day my essence is diminished,
when this season of impending change
has pushed me to the limit.

In the distance I hear the bus roar,
see its dim lights close to Fort Lee Road.
I could shirk this destiny,
retreat to the shelter, deferential, cowardly,
but I don't.

The bus comes closer.
I take a deep breath, see it's the express,
muster my courage, and stiffen my right arm,
lifting it into the morning darkness.
The bus appears at first to defy me
as the engine surges.
A wave of shame blows through my porous soul.
I feel invisible,
an unimportant thing. . .
like a November leaf.

I'm giving way to doubts, tell myself,
"The bus is going to blow past us."
Then I hear the engine throttle down,
and it eases toward the curb,
halting in front of me in a montage
of moans and shrieks.

I climb on.
The west wind seems to lift me up
the first step.
The bus has stopped because of me,

because I thrust my arm
into the air on this murky November morning.

What power!
I do matter.
I am not invisible.
I'm no November leaf.

Lunar Eclipse

(riding the 166 bus from New York to Leonia)

I often sleep on the bus
on the way back to New Jersey.
New York City drains each bit of energy
from you, you know:
The hectic walk to the bus in the chilly morning darkness,
wondering if you have your bus pass;
sitting next to a stranger each day on the 166;
ascending and descending stairs in Port Authority;
racing through the city streets, watching your back, front,
either side, only to do it all again on the way home.
And that's just coming and going.

What about the work?
It is no longer good enough to just show up.
Companies expecting things for their money
nowadays in this economy.

But tonight as we came up out of the Lincoln Tunnel
on the way home,
I looked toward the Manhattan skyline
and saw a bright, full moon
watching over the sleepless city.
The brightness even hovered on the Hudson,
casting a glassy sheen
on a sliver of the black water below.

After I saw this, I tried to fall asleep on the bus
but could not help but think
about the beauty

I had seen in the eastern sky.
I was still lost in those thoughts
as we reached familiar sights
approaching the New Jersey Turnpike,
yet the eastern radiance just would not let me go.

Had I just glimpsed the face of God
watching over a forsaken city?
I don't know.
In hours, the lunar eclipse will hide
the moonglow
and doubts will descend.

Winter

First Weekend of December

(inspired by an early December walk in the woods at Flat Rock Brook Nature Center in Englewood, New Jersey)

The trees have finished their autumn striptease
and tower over me
naked, unashamed.

Icy winds will soon descend on us,
signaling the start of snowy pristine beauty.
For a while we'll be content,
but you can only stand the icy cold
for so long till you long for warmth
and golden summer days.

Winter woos you with her beauty,
but over time her icy stare, gray sky,
and endless chill make you long for something else,
for anything.

Shoveling Snow

If a man should die while shoveling snow,
this would not be how he wished to go.

He would not croak doing what he loved,
wearing a couple of unmatched gloves—
both for the left hand.

Death by shoveling is for men up North.
They look outside and must go forth.
Jumping out of the easy chair,
struggling into long underwear,
attacking the first big snowfall of the year,
a gladiator in his winter gear,
an aging man living on the edge
while guys down South trim hedges
in their short-sleeved, floral prints.

The truth is: Men up North die in winter boots,
men down South in their birthday suits.

A man hopes to die while making love.
This would be a gift from above.
For a Northern man to go this way,
he has to relocate to Tampa Bay
or spend his winters down in Cocoa Beach
to bring the dream within his reach.

But if a man should die while shoveling snow,
this would not be how he wished to go.

'Tis The Season

Christmas circumvents the Savior
for a lot of profligate behavior.
Spending sprees by families
unable to restrain themselves
despite all homilies on self-restraint
urging the faithful not to taint
the blessed name of the first Saint from elsewhere.

I hear the sound of angels singing
drowned out by cash registers a-ringing.

'Twas the Soccer Practice Before Christmas

The daughters of privilege are practicing soccer
in the gym at the Leonia Middle School
on December 22nd
while the daughters of desolation are hoping
they will get something for Christmas this year,
wondering if Dad will stop by for a visit,
thinking he might not be acting right again,
certain he will not have any money to buy gifts,
hoping against hope anyway
because that is all they have.

Waiting for Easter

Snow descended for the annual family picture last Thursday
with people sitting upright
on prickly evergreen branches,
posing for next year's Christmas cards,
reminding the world that Norman Rockwell is no more.

Snow can be like that—
flaunting beauty in pure-white velvet gowns
just before the coming Lenten deprivation,
when self-denial strides in step
with the dearth of wildflowers and honeysuckle.

In the end, spring always comes,
Easter always eclipses Lenten longings
with its Resurrection,
world without end.

O Come Passover, O Come Easter

Ancient boulders, steady and secure:
Barren winter trees upon their shoulders,
precarious,
daring,
reach across the vast divide.

Ice-capped crystal water
bubbles below,
waiting for summer
to dismiss the dismal gray
and banish it until the next Solstice
or until Thanksgiving next at least
or Armistice or, say, Election Day.

O come, Passover with your lengthening days.
O come, Easter with your hopeful sunrise,
your marvelous blue skies.

Thoughts of Moving Home

(when I'm in my hometown of Mount Vernon, Illinois,
I always think about moving back there)

Last week, nine degrees and icy cold;
today, seventy-two and warm.
But the sky remains gray all the same
and the pull to return is always there—
back to my people,
my pace,
our relatives.

Only the last names are the same now.
The first have changed,
stepping aside for a new generation
that also calls me to come home.

Is it nostalgia stirring this desire?
Are glory days of youth beckoning me back?
Is it the rugged unforgiving flatlands
that I want to roam once more?
Is it a challenge, something to be conquered,
or a chance to start again?

We left, we proved that we could make it out there,
out East, out in that great big shadow of New York.
Should we come home
to prove we can make it here?

Spring

∾

Spring Awakening

Spring awakening
turns me into a dervish of activity—

act now, analyze later
is the mantra made for me
come April.

Do and do, do and do,
are what I do when weather warms.

I think in winter.
Therefore, I'm not thinking now.

Longing for Stillness

The brook has these glorious stretches of stillness
that only last for moments.
Then a blockade of boulders suddenly appears;
narrowing passageways of whooshing water
take some skillful navigation
to the next expanse of calm.
Many fail at this and find themselves
adrift in time,
perched on craggy rocks
and waiting for the next big rain to come
and raise the water far enough
to push them back downstream.

Dry times are the worst,
and some poor things just sit there
on a rock in the brook,
marking time, hoping against hope
for a rainy day
even though April showers
have given way to May
and a dry, thirsty summer lies in wait.

Maybe someone
will shove a stick down in the water,
give that still-green leaf a little nudge
to get it moving once again
while chipmunks scurry in the shade,
beneath the chatter of the birds.

I Went for a Walk at Flat Rock Brook

The farther I went among the trees
at Flat Rock Brook,
the louder the roar
on the path I took.

The water raged over boulders
deep in the woods,
but when it neared the neighborhood,
it suddenly grew peaceful and serene.

I am not like the brook, mild-mannered—
I rant and rave
in the neighborhood.
But the deeper I go into the woods,
the more at peace I am.

I left on a Saturday in March;
low-lying clouds hung over me,
indifferent to my stroll.
But as I prayed for this and that,
those emissaries of the winter fled,
releasing me into a burst of bright spring light.

Did You See the Sun?

Did you see the sun rise today
up, up, up to noon?
Yesterday I thought it might
never overtake the night.
And not so very long ago,
I thought that I might never see its glow.

Then
the next day it was up, up, up again
shining, shining, shining.

Did you see the Son risen today
up, up, up to noon?
Yesterday I thought He might
never overtake my night.
And not so very long ago,
I thought I might never see His glow.

Then
the next day He was up, up, up again
shining, shining, shining.

Easter Laughter

Easter Sunday: Look outside.
Birds sing; spring is alive.
Wear something bright,
something new.
Celebrate—
have another cup of coffee.
Feast on
things extraordinary.
Laugh at
death and graves
that will not hold us down
forever.

Ode to Morning in May

Just before dawn,
I step outside in May
and hear them.

The birds chatter away,
cacophonous to me,
news and gossip to them.

I step inside
and shut the door
on the world outside.
The coffee pot moans in labor
in the kitchen,
brightening another day's journey
with her liquid love.

The Coliseum

(watching an indoor soccer game at the Teaneck Coliseum)

The coliseum of the enfranchised
teemed with the tyrants of tomorrow.
Soccer moms with sagging bodies,
taxi drivers transporting the gifted and talented
to private tutors and private lessons
paid for by the hour
with the ill-gotten gain of corporate America,

children whose maxed-out mediocrity
appears as a mirage of greatness,
only to descend to Earth in time—
not in a crash or boom or in a fiery descent
but gently, on a golden parachute,
fluttering like a cat that always lands
upright on his feet when kicked,

while the coliseum of the disenfranchised idly sits by,
waiting to be told what to do.
This is all they know.

All

Joseph's empty tomb,
Earth's empty womb,
Jesus
delivered up for us all—

not one, not some,
not just a few,
but all.

Everyman, everywoman,
John Doe, Jane Doe,
superheroes, extraordinaries,
even less than ordinaries,
all,

Jews and Gentiles,
and even those god-awful pedophiles,
every last one, all.

Summer

Second-Home Boulevard
at the Jersey Shore

Boats lie at anchor
just behind Second-Home Boulevard,
where the mighty maintain surplus stuff
and weekend getaway places of refuge
while the also-rans stay home
and wait for the carnival to come to town.

Then they can get out of their apartments
for a few hours
to buy some cotton candy.

Sense of Direction

We came to stay at Barnegat Bay,
spending a lazy day at Island Beach Park,
ending with an evening barbeque
midway through summer break
at the end of July.

The haze hovered as it had
the day JFK Junior flew his Cessna
almost back to the Vineyard ten years ago—
almost to the day, the fateful day,
when he lost his sense of direction.

Summer's like that.
You lose your bearings
and lack routine.
The rhythms of life are interrupted
by the background sound
of ocean waves and longer days
and managing exposure to the sun
till the first day of school.

You remember that this kind of day seems normal,
not that lying in the sun,
alternately napping and reading the book
you never have time for any other time of year.

Summer's one brief glimpse
at the boundless beauty of eternity,
a sneak preview of days to come,

where there is rest in God's unbound expanse.

Until then, teach us to number our days
and our summer lilies
and cherish what's to come.

Flip-Flop Nation

We wear flip-flops way too much.
A nation great as ours can't stay as such
when we walk around without our shoes.
This flip-flop nation gives me the blues.

Flip-flops are leisure footwear,
not made for running:
No protection found there.
Barefoot people live in the Third World,
their flags in tatters when they are unfurled.
"America is great because she's good."
But would de Tocqueville thus have spoken
if he'd seen flip-flops in Hollywood?

Flip-flops are a shoe for the lazy.
I do not exaggerate;
I am not crazy.
Our nation's security has a gaping breach.
Flip-flops used to be an item for the beach.
Now we wear them in January
to the grocery store.

Flip-flopped people are not prepared for war.
They walk around slowly,
shuffle across the floor.
I guarantee the Russians are not doing this.

Flip-flops don't support our arches.
They flatten our feet,
leave us incapable of military marches

or engaging enemies behind front lines.

To me these flip-flops are a certain sign
because flip-flops and greatness don't align.

Barbeque Grill

My grill, my manhood:
oh, the thrill
of lighting the barbeque grill.
The sizzle of the meat,
fire, smoke:
This is not a joke.
I take a pyrotechnic joy
in lighting up propane.
It sounds insane.

The suburban hunter-gatherer makes
a prehistoric journey every time
he turns on the grill,
in his mind tracking the prey all the way
to the fateful moment
when manly triumph lies there on display,

the lighting of the grill penultimate
before the victor's venison's unveiled.
Holy fire purifies the offering of the primal priest
who has prepared the feast.
Smoke signals rising in the sky
identify the chief,
the guy upon whose grill
the metamorphosis of meat
will soon turn into tasty morsels,
rugged glory.

Nature

The Beauty of Rain

Sometimes the rain dives straight down from the sky.
Sometimes sideways it seems to fall.
Give me these gray skies any day
over an unimpeded golden sun.

Rain keeps me calm,
unbound by thoughts of what
I've failed to do in life.

I can justify sitting and looking
out a window on a rainy day,
but not when brightness
blazes down on me at noon.
"Do something!" the sky seems to scream on those days.
The pressure builds inside my chest.
I am among the masses living life in quiet desperation,
except when it rains and I relax
and think about how beautiful the rain is
when it falls.

Bounty

Nature's bounty beckons wired suburbanites
who make their money in the concrete jungles,
bewildered by another kind of wealth in boulevards
where all converge
to step right over those who can't keep up—

Darwin's fittest rise to untold riches—
the rest adapting to whatever fate
befalls their lack of skill.

Would hurried humans choose that life
if they could sit beside a brook
and listen to the water?
Would they remain in this perpetual pursuit
after ten minutes watching chipmunks
glide across craggy rocks
while solitary golden leaves,
lifted from lofty branches,
flutter away?

Some plunder the concrete jungle,
escaping home in daily drab commutes.
Others lose their souls,
unable to let go of the pursuit
of their elusive bounty.

Soaring

My spirit soars amid the sound of water.
These woods lift my soul
out of the doldrums of my daily life.
When I walk along these leafy trails,
my belief in God grows larger.
Here, He seems more real than anything.

The world's hold on me weakens,
its unrelenting grasp starts to give way.
I'm free again:
Oppressive thoughts of all I have to do
dissipate into light cumulous
hovering overhead in endless sky.

Hope returns.
Despair departs,
cowering for cover
in the face of so much loveliness;
mental anguish trembles;
a thousand sounds of life drowned out
by drudgery of daily duty
rise again.

Still

The sound of the water in Flat Rock Brook
whipping past age-old boulders
circles me with calm,
makes me forget awhile
the daily commute to New York
beginning with the race to the bus stop,
to find standing-room only,
to be tortured by screeching brakes
in stop-and-go traffic
and cell phone ringtones of people
who believe their conversations
are the only ones that matter.

The brook unties the knots around my stomach.
My jaw relaxes as the water glides.

My mind tells me relaxing's wrong and ruinous.
I tense up, guilty that I'm not achieving
anything right now
but sitting in one place.
The steady hum says,
"Shhhh, be still."

Healing Woods

Healing woods—
where songbird duets lift despair
into the air,
chasing sounds towards altitudes
far beyond gloomy oppression;

healing woods—
where the sound of water's
like the voice of God,
suppressing self-destructive thoughts
and voices of the vain
who strive for shiny things
tomorrow's toys will trump
in an endless show of unrewarding days;

healing woods—
where ancient boulders hold their secrets
of people who never imagined
a world without walls,
where everything is right in front of them
on a smart phone,
that little conduit of all of the world's anxiety,
addling the minds of millions
who cannot imagine
where this electronic age will end up;

healing woods—
woo us with nature's wisdom
and steady, circular seasons of life

while the world is strapped
to the back of a missile
shooting who knows where,
not looking back.

Family

Ill Conceived

I was ill conceived—
lust,
passion,
random chance
in the backseat
of a Chevrolet,
late December '63,
a Saturday
during the period of mourning
for President Kennedy.

I was ill received—
by a father
(what a bother,
take him hither,
leave me yonder;
thus he went).
Little did I know
he wouldn't come again:
More oats he would sow
(and what about your baby boy,
your baby boy?).

Leave me be, my little boy.
You were not even meant to be.
I want to live.
I want to roam
this fertile land of liberty.

I always wondered why you left.
Did you see me first and then decide?
Or was it sight unseen?
Either way, an unseemly sight,
a permanently crippling blight.

Was it my face, my eyes, my hair?
Did I cry too much?
Sigh too much?
Sleep too much?
Was my skin too light and fair?

Tell me now, before you die.
Tell me now, before I cry.
Tell me, say, what did I do?
Tell me, say, whatever's true.

Son, I never even thought of you.

Leaving LaGuardia for a Funeral

No room for error leaving LaGuardia,
the water's edge marking the end of second chances
just beyond the runway.
The plane barely lifts up off the ground.
We rise, and I relax a little but not much.
I'm right above engine, wondering where
Canadian geese are at this time of year
since the weather's getting warmer.

Sully retired two weeks ago.
Without him, what are the chances
of a second Miracle on the Hudson
or the Harlem River or Flushing Bay?
About the same as another
Olympic Miracle on Ice, I'd say.

The plane banks to the right.
I see Archie Bunker's neighborhood
in working-class Queens.
George Jefferson's deluxe apartment in the sky
is somewhere down there, too.

In the distance, I can see Manhattan also
on this foggy day in March.
The skyline glistens near the Empire State,
sun peeking through the haze.

My eyes range south,
looking again for the Towers of Babel

as I always do when the city is in view.
They're still not there.
Moloch's demolition remains irreversible.

The sun works its way slowly south,
but downtown's just beyond the spreading rays.
Lower Manhattan suspended in darkness still.
Oh, how the mighty have fallen.
Sadness has settled on the faces of the buildings,
the burden of loss still visible
under the veils of darkness.

I am going to my grandma's funeral today.

I Left My Grandpa Sitting in the Recliner

(on the flight home after spending five days with my grandpa after the death of my grandma)

I left my grandpa crying
in the burgundy recliner,
first-time widower after seventy-one years,
wondering
how he could live without her,

thinking
he wouldn't be able to do it,
telling me
he might not be there
when I came home to visit him in June.

Sleeping
in the chair or couch at night
so he wouldn't have to climb into the bed alone
or soil the sheets he'd shared with her,

rising
in faith when he sang the hymn to himself,
"I've Anchored My Soul
In the Haven of Rest,"
even the verses,

drowning
in despair when he realized
how much he missed her
on that damp and dreary day in March,

remembering
how he'd lost his dad
when he was just eleven.

But nothing is like this.
Everything
has changed,
will never be
the way it was again.

Something will happen to my grandpa
and your grandpa
and you
and me,
maybe sometime soon.

I left my grandpa crying
in the burgundy recliner,
wishing
he had gotten the new carpeting
in the living room
that she wanted long ago.

The old brown carpet will be good enough
for the now
while he sits in the burgundy recliner,
crying,
sleeping,
waiting
for something.

Father's Day and Not One Thought

Father's Day,
and not one thought
of the man who brought me
into this world.

And not once did I say,
"Dad, I miss you today."

And not one contemplation
of the man who made me
feel so small
as if I did not count for him at all.

Father's Day
is just that way for me.
No longer guilty
that I didn't send
a token card or note.

I wish that I could say
I miss him on this day.
But I can't and won't
because I don't.

I miss the idea
of having a dad—
that's what makes me sad.
Otherwise, this burden's
not so bad.

Midwesterners

A peaceful Midwestern pace
calls me to come home
where people have more space,
where the feel is not frenetic,
frantic, fighting daily wars for parking places
and shareholder value,

where the land's not overprocessed,
egos not enveloped
in their own importance,
where children are not mere extensions
of their parents' hunger after prominence,

where men relax and are at ease
with hands slipped into blue-jean pockets,
waiting for their women to tell them what to do.

People of the plains just aren't purpose-driven,
Blackberry-toting, Burberry-bagged,
Starbucks-caffeinated people.

Let the movers and shakers move and shake
and take their migraine medicine
while mild-mannered Midwesterners manage
America's fruited plains and open spaces.

We Gather Together and Come Apart

We gather together
and come apart.
This is what we do,
no matter what.
The joy of connectedness
is something to behold,
but then we come unraveled:
This is what gets old.

Life seems to do it
by fighting us all the way.
We try to be family
but cannot stay.
We always end up me
or at the very least myself and I.
We start out all together,
then degenerate to my.

And so I stop to breathe,
resign myself to sigh,
and wonder whatever happened to
"Day is done,
God is nigh?"
I feel better
when I hear that lullaby.

My Wife Is Not a Morning Person

My wife is not a morning person,
but she still creates a kinesthetic fuss
before the sun comes up,
walking in pitter-patter steps
 across the hardwood floors—
into the shower,
out of the shower.
Then comes more pitter-patter,
and other kinds of clatter,
while I sit and read beneath a solitary light.

Down the stairs she comes,
basket of dirty laundry in her hands.
The concrete basement floors
cause me to lose all track of her,
the creaky wooden ones like GPS.
Soon the water in the washer's running;
she ascends the stairs,
staccato steps tracking her again,
bearing a white basket of clean laundry.

Before I know it, she descends the stairs again
at Mach One, dressed for the day,
to make lunches, let loose some loud commands
to dilly-dallying daughters who don't hurry,
all too aware of the aberration of their fate
that means their mom
teaches at the school where they attend.

Why us? It is so cosmically unfair to girls
who know that teachers get to school
forty-five minutes early
every day.

I stay out of the way.

The women rumble through the back door
one by one, following the leader.
Shifting into reverse, the van speeds backwards
in a burst toward the street.
Good thing you cannot get a speeding ticket
in your driveway, or she might,
every day.
I'm serious.

The suburban soccer-mom minivan
soon's out of sight.
I take a deep and cleansing breath,
commotion gone,
stillness returning.

You may, I know, not quite believe
my wife is not a morning person.

I'm not kidding.

Loved

I was loved when I was small
even though my dad was never there at all.
He left my mom when I was two.
Is that what a man's supposed to do?

Like Jack, Jack, Kerouac,
he went on the road and never looked back,
sowed wild oats,
played slide trombone,
paid no alimony,
called not ever on the phone.

Yet I was loved when I was small.
Yes, I was loved when I was small.

Fondue

(for Marcia's forty-second birthday)

I have loved you for a long while;
then I learned you share
the birthday of Bill Strunk, of Strunk and White,
The Elements of Style.
I think I love you even more now.

Then I learned your birthday is the same day
Darwin first presented evolution publicly.
I love you, anyway.

Then I saw you shared the birthday of Princess Di,
the one who died the week after
we moved into the first house we ever owned,
the one with central air.
I miss it there
on Christie Lane
when summer's here
on Westview.
But I love you, yes, I do—
And may love fondue, too.

Today is the first day of July.
Look around, up in the sky.
See the beauty and believe it's true.
You've finally got to forty-two.
Maybe tonight we can share some fondue.

Almost

(for Rachel on her 13th birthday)

You were almost born
in New York City,
near Chinatown.
Being from the Midwest,
your Aunt Carol wanted a cappuccino
and a cannoli,
things you cannot find
in Southern Illinois.
Your mother, always a gracious host,
endured her labor pains
at a sidewalk cafe
in Little Italy.

You were almost born
on the George Washington Bridge.
Your mother had gotten really quiet
on the West Side Highway.
The other women grew suspicious,
men up front oblivious
to the secrets of Eve's sisterhood.
The traffic was light
on the night of May the 7th.
We managed to drop them off
at our apartment in Cliffside Park.

You were almost born
on Fort Lee Road.
"Chris, go faster!"
A squad car pulled us over for speeding

through a red light
at the Glenwood Avenue intersection
in Leonia.
"Chris, hurry!"
I jumped out of the car,
right in front of the upholstery shop.
"Sir, stop! Get back in your car!"
"Officer, my wife is having a baby!"
"Are you serious?"
"Yes!"
He must have looked back, seen your mother
with her eyes rolled back in her head,
moaning.
"Follow me! I'll take you there!"
He did not ask me where.
There was no time for small talk.

You could have been born
at any number of places:
Overpeck Park,
the Marriott at Glenpointe,
an Exxon station,
the hospital parking lot.
But your mother held her knees together
so you'd have a proper birthplace,
not like your namesake in the Bible—
the matriarch Rachel,
who had her son Benjamin
by the side of the road.

You were born in Holy Name Hospital
after Dr. Ajjan met us at the door
of the emergency room.

He wheeled you up to the birthing room himself,
special delivery.
No time to stick an IV in your mother's arm,
to ask about insurance,
pace the floor, and wait for full dilation.
No time for any of that.

You came out cranky
when you were born.
This made me think
you wished that it had happened
in New York
on Sunday night:
May 7th.

It almost did.

Byron Was Buried
the Day Jacko Died

Byron was buried the day Jacko died.
One known in few places, one known worldwide.
Both had hearts that gave way in an instant.
I think this is ironic.
If not, what is it?

My dad died the same day as Coretta Scott King.
This, too, is a peculiar thing.
How did it happen?
What does it mean?

I remember the night in the Gateway Hotel,
Michael moonwalked on Motown's
twenty-fifth anniversary special.
My room was on the twenty-fifth floor.
This was the day before
I left for the Marine Corps.
The same night my grandpa
was propositioned by a whore
in the hotel lobby.
He was angry and rushed out
the revolving front door.
Then they left me all alone,
at nineteen, in St. Louis,
at a hotel that isn't there anymore.

They drove away
in a brown Mercury Marquis—

going home, my mom and girlfriend
looking out of the rear window at me,
crying until they crossed
the Mississippi,
leaving Missouri to let me start
my journey into manhood
while they went back into Illinois.

This was before the floating casinos
lit up the water at night,
when all you could see
was the black of the water below.

I had stood at the street corner,
told them to go.
I couldn't cry.
I wondered why I was doing this,
and still can't tell you to this day.
But I now know that was the night
I left Byron and boyhood dreams behind.

Not much later, he left town, too.
I wish this next part were not true,
but it is.

I only saw him one more time
after the night Michael danced.
Once.

This was not intentional.
I don't know how it happened.
But it did.

Next thing you know,
Byron's buried the day Jacko died.
You might have guessed the next part:
I only cried
once.

This was not intentional either.

Faith

Whisper

So many associate God with noise—
great acts of nature,
standing ovations, encores,
jagged mountains crossing the horizon.

But Elijah found God in stillness.
Heard His voice in a whisper,
the way your best friend cups her hands
around her mouth and tells you a secret
up close in your ear.

Morning

I awake and walk downstairs
toward the smell of coffee,
where I'll find, somewhere in the living room,
another sign the cat is dying—
a hairy mixture heaved up
sometime before sunrise.

It's one sure sign
she's getting ready for that day
because it happens every morning,
just like those others
who have bodies
that are giving way.
Through the night,
they heave and hurl their sins away,
hoping God removes all traces of their shame
just as I do for that kitty
come morning.

Apples

I cannot seem to remove the stickers
that they put on apples nowadays:
My nails are gnawed too short
to flick the edge up so that I can pull it off.
Epic struggles have ensued between
a Golden Delicious and me—
angry exchanges between the natural man
and nature's best.

Several times, it seems,
the stickers actually have hunkered down.
I've grabbed a paring knife;
the sticker has grown obstinate,
daring me to do my worst.
I soon concede defeat
and cut deep under it
and through the skin.

This drastic measure
leaves a crater on the surface
that will turn brown in my lunch bag
and be unbecoming in an apple.

Maybe it knows its fate
and figures it should fight
until all hope is lost.

Some sins are like this—
stubborn and not easily removed.

Finally, you have to take some drastic measures
to remove the things.
Sometimes the removal leaves a divot
in the soul that will not go away.

Maybe the sin knows its fate too,
so it holds on till Judgment Day
or Baptism, or a walk in the woods
that makes it vulnerable
and it lets go.

Tsunami

Most days sadness slowly seeps into my soul.
I manage modest sums like this—
feel their dull ache but am otherwise unmoved.

Daily doses of accomplishment, of piety, of prayer,
family, and friends suppress the sadness,
though, and blunt its force.

Today a real tsunami of it slammed me,
cascading over me
and turning my attentive gaze
into a blank stare.

A massive wall of sadness walloped me,
and faith fell flat.

One moment life's a fairy tale,
the next a cautionary script
wallowing in murky dark.

The Confession of Joan Didion

The confession of Joan Didion
along with her husband, John Gregory Dunne,
was that neither one
believed in the Resurrection—

He a Catholic,
she Episcopalian,
but neither for the Resurrection.

Death is the end.
Everything turns white.
This was what she said.
This is what she writes
in her Year of Magical Thinking.

But where's the magic
absent the Resurrection?

Manly Worship

So heaven meets earth like a sloppy wet kiss
and my heart turns violently inside of my chest.

—John Mark McMillan, "How He Loves"

We need worship songs for guys
with lyrics about meat, ketchup, and fries.
Why these songs about feelings and stuff,
all this namby-pamby fluff?

We need worship songs for men.
The songs we sing are too feminine.
Too much emotion, and too much goo—
I want a song with spicy barbeque.

Our worship is romantic comedy;
I'm out of sorts before the homily.
I want to worship God on high
with something relevant to a guy.

This is a church with manly men,
but we're singing girly songs again.
Let's sing songs that stir us machos,
songs with extra cheese and nachos.

I'm sick of huggy, kissy Lord.
I feel like such a sissy, Lord.
I want a song fit for a ranch,
or driving eighty in an Avalanche.

If I hear one more song about your touch,
I think I'm going to lose my lunch.
I want a song I can sing with a torch,
lyrics where the earth gets scorched.
Don't want to sing 'bout a kiss from your lips.

Why not do Apocalypse?

No Better Place

There is no better place to be
than in the house of God.

Are you sure?
Have you ever
sat by the window in a coffee shop
with a latte on rainy day?
Have you walked
in the woods in April
when the honeysuckle
hovers in the air
and fills your mind
with recollections of a time
when the world was a magic place?

Sometimes my heart
longs for those sanctuaries,
not this one.

Have you gone to a place
where a child's face
lights with joy when she receives
the ice cream cone from the man
with the silver spoon?

Sometimes there's no better place
to be in the world
than . . . there.

Relationships

Closeness Is Elusive

Closeness is elusive.
You might even call it reclusive.

Chasing after three days of piled-up dirty laundry
that will not let you forget its burden
until you finish those eight loads
and throw away every stray softener sheet
before racing after your eight-year-old boy's
travel baseball team
as they traverse green and brown diamonds
all over creation, when you realize
you deferred your own dreams long ago to his.

You look, and what was once your lover
is now not quite a stranger, more a
co-worker in a parenting business,
making sure the golden child
has all the opportunities
you did not have.

Now the last thing you *did* have—
this closeness of two hearts entwined—
is slipping from you as the boy
wonders what he'll get to do tomorrow

and you remember what you had so long ago.

My Fault Is the Default

My fault is the default,
the place we always start;
and then we move to Shut Down—
that's the hardest part:

Silence—
looking the other way,
turning the other cheek,
ignoring the chance to love,
to resolve, to repair.

Dissolving—
into terse remarks,
stiff hearts adrift
in an ever-widening sea;

dancing—
a solo dance
together
in a parallel universe.
Unwilling to chance,
to risk,
to converse.

My fault is the default,
the place we always start
and then we move to Shut Down.

Will we ever choose Restart?

Lost Love

We lost our love and cannot find it.
I think it happened in our first apartment,
the one on Waverly Avenue, but I'm not sure.
It was a hot August night,
and we slept with the windows open
and a dusty oscillating fan
that kept on going back and forth.
You said you hadn't slept at all that night.
If not there, where?

It might have been the house
we rented on Cherry Lane.
I remember the night when I thought
I heard our love go down the drain,
swirling and gurgling
until that final sucking sound
said love had left us.
If not there, where?

It's hard to tell
because there was also the night
in our first house on Thirty-fifth Street.
You nudged me
to get up and take care of the baby.
I said I had to get my sleep,
so I could go to work the next day.
You screamed and scampered across the floor,
digging in your heels for emphasis
on the creaky hardwood,

calling me unthinkable things,
things I still remember six years later.
Every single word.
If not there, where?

Some say you cannot really
lose love in this manner,
on a Thursday evening, all at once.

Coffee

I love the sound of coffee
when it's poured into a cup.
Even though I'm only ten years old,
I do not make this up:
Percolating liquid in a pot,
moaning and groaning in ecstasy,
is a glorious sound to me.

When I grow up,
I can only hope getting married
will be as wonderful as coffee.

Size Matters

I see a lot of big women
who marry a little man,
seemingly to boss him around—
this seems to be the plan.

Same thing goes for those young women
who marry older men.
He probably has money,
but, otherwise,
she is directing him.

Same thing goes for the beauty
who marries an ugly man.
About this I can guarantee
(I say with total certainty):
She'll lead him by the hand.

I guess that even little women
who marry big tall men
soon bark their orders from below:
Stature certainly has no effect
on one's ability to dominate
the man who lets her run the show.

Self

Nails

People think I'm laid back, easy-going,
but I'm not so sure.
Look at my fingernails.
I've been gnawing on them now
for forty years—
maybe even longer.

I've stopped gnawing several times for naught.
I always go back to them.
Nervous gnawing never seems to end
for more than a day or two.
Next thing you know
something's weighing in on me,
and I go at it once again.

Not cigarettes or chewing gum,
potato chips or chocolate bars,
or peanut butter from the jar—
finger nails:

A victimless vice of unvanity.
Not a secret—
how can it be?
These hands tell the story for anyone
who looks at me
with more than a passing glance.

My fingernails announce some deeper meaning
I still hope to find.

Beautiful Us

Back when we were innocent,
I wonder where it went.
Let's go back and find it.

—Bon Jovi, "When We Were Beautiful"

We were beautiful in our day,
but over the years our beauty gives way
to a thousand vices
and overzealous vanities
while we stay up too late,
squeezing every minute out of every day
while galaxies light up the night sky.
"If I'd known I was going to live this long,
I would have taken better care of myself."
We all say this.

Some surrender beauty to career,
others to Twinkies,
others still to feeling better every day.

Some are aged by nervousness,
others by guilt and shame.
Beauty does not leave us in a cataclysmic exodus.
It slips away while we're asleep,
melts in the midday sun.

We wash our faces
and apply our moisturizers
before we turn the night light off,

only to realize in the morning
that we can't recapture what we had
when we were beautiful.

Unravel

Sometimes I unravel slowly,
other times all at once.
But always I unravel,
somehow, unravel I must.

I grow tense when it makes no sense,
grow weary when I should be cheery.
I grow anxious and antsy
and this is no fancy.
It is on my face,
surrounding any place
I dwell in.

I un-
rav-
el.

Sadness Clings to Me

Sadness clings to me sometimes.
It comes after nightfall
and follows me to bed
and climbs under the covers with me.

I awake to find it still there.
I shower, but no matter
how hard I scrub with soap or shampoo,
the sadness remains in my skin
and hair and everywhere else I look.

The mirror does not lie.
I look older with a sadness on my face
that fills my soul,
welling up in waterlogged eyes,
distorting my view of Easter lilies.

Sometimes sadness clings to me
like the pink Cling Free
that clung to my grandfather's pant leg once.

It was visible from behind,
just below the cuff on his work pants,
sticking to the back of the boots
he wore to lay brick,
held fast there all day
though he was unaware.
My mother thought
this was the funniest thing in the world.

Some people are unaware of their sadness,
but look closely and you will see it there.
Others feel sadness thickening over them
and cannot move anywhere.

Either way, this sadness clings to me.

I Deify Me

I deify Me.
This foolish elevation
of self
does not satisfy,
cannot satisfy,
will not satisfy
this foolish degradation
of You.

I deify Me.
Despite your warning,
no other images,
no other gods—
I go on ignoring.

Still I deify Me.
Still I defy You.

Work

Shareholder Value

I gave my life to the corporation
and then I did retire.
Created all kinds of shareholder value—
thus did I aspire.
In the end,
I received a pension
and an honorable mention
in the company's newsletter.

Never took time for walks in the woods,
yet provided my family the greatest of goods,
vacationed in villas in Mexico,
kept up with the P/E ratio—
though I couldn't possibly let go,
of email and voicemail in Puerto Vallerto.
And what for this do I have to show?
Here: a mahogany, gold-plated memento.

If I could go back
and do it again
I'd leave work on time
and stand in line
with my kids for ice cream cones.

UPS Man on the Upper East Side

*(at a Starbucks on the Upper East Side of New York City
while I was wearing UPS browns)*

I deliver packages on the Upper East Side—
designer purses,
none from Naugahyde.
I smile at all the doormen,
yet at the end of day,
my body aches
and o my mind feels nothing but dismay.

I'm the UPS man
dressed in pullman brown.
Sometimes this entire gig
can work a man way down.

I'm a Teamster in a truck,
some blue-collar guy
delivering the stuff all day
that I could never buy.

Human Resources

Each day, I pass through guarded gates
to enter the house of Resources Human
to utilize my time on tasks,
detailed in lengthy project plans
created by the man
who sits in the high-back chair
in the corner office
while I wear pleated pants
and a sports coat,
tethered to a hands-free headset
so I can talk
in cross-functional conference calls
with colleagues
in cubicles across the enterprise.

I unleash myself and walk over
to look outside the window:
There, the corporate campus,
sprawling in suburbia:
manicured grass,
leaves discarded,
unblemished,
totally unreal.

The Parking Lot Flag Man
on 62nd Street

I wave my flag the whole day long.
My right arm soon grows weary;
I switch to the left.

Cars seem to ignore my flag
when I wave with the left hand—
same one our recent Presidents used
to sign those bills.

Two fifteen-minute breaks and a half-hour lunch—
the rest of the time I wave the red flag,
hoping folks will park in our garage.
I do not think it matters.

Man, it's a job.

The people who walk by never look at me.
They look right through me
and my flag.

Modernity

I'm Still Alone

I tweet on Twitter to cyberspace.
I blog on Blogger to state my case.
I look at Facebook and see my friends—
more than three-hundred and fifty and ten.

This is the virtual world we now live in.
But let me state a remarkable fact:
I'm still alone.

The computer's the only thing I see:
All of these soulless images looking back at me.
Tweets and statuses, blogs and such,
yet no other person has felt my touch.

I'm now connected to all of the world
but this does not change a remarkable fact:
I'm still alone.

New World Order

Superficiality is the curse of our age.
—Richard Foster, The Celebration
of Discipline, 1978.

Choices, decisions, are weighing me down,
my mind is overwhelmed.
Forty flavors of ice cream,
twenty-nine kinds of coffee
in three sizes—that mean something
completely different than you would think.

Costco has nearly everything in bulk.
Amazon has everything period,
and you can find it in .05 seconds—
even the first Jackson Browne album ever made.

No one throws anything away.
When they get done with it,
they sell it on eBay.

I wish the world would
just slow down and breathe—
a deep, cleansing breath.
Let's talk about this
and decide if it's really what we want:
this virtual world.

Email's way too slow,
so you IM me.

But I'm not there,
so you call me on the phone.
But I am already on the phone,
so you text me
because you know I'm too busy
to listen to my voice mail.

Is this what we all want?
This millisecond world
where I only get a few seconds
to make life's most important decisions?

Revolution 2.0

I thought I understood
how the world was going to end.
Now I'm not so sure.

The world is upside down.
Turmoil's touring the Middle East,
cutting-edge confusion
running on the latest operating systems.
Tunisia, Egypt, Libya,
Twitter, Facebook, Google:
weapons of mass revolution.

Tiananmen Square would have fared
differently had Twitter been there.
A tank is no match for a tweet
in this new world order.
One little post with a #hashtag
will turn into twenty-thousand tweets
in twenty minutes.
Next thing you know,
ten thousand people will be standing
in front of your presidential palace,
daring the bullies to shoot them
with rubber bullets.

Go viral, and victory will follow.
The Art of War is no more
what it was.
Everything has changed.

You say you want a revolution?
Smart bombs have stepped aside.
Smart phones and mobile apps
mobilize the masses,
who tell the dictator to disappear.
Give him a few days, and he will—
after he moves his billions
out of Swiss bank accounts
and his mistresses to seaside villas.

On the Origins of Beat Poetry

I started reading an anthology of the Beat Poets.
Loved the one by the woman whose husband
kept ruining her moments of inspiration
by asking her to do practical things
like call the insurance people.

Noticed they liked to mention leaky faucets.
I have a hunch.
This may sound dumb,
but if Ginsberg had known anything about plumbing,
the whole thing might never have happened.

Various Endings

Not the Pastor Anymore

(in Allison Park, Englewood Cliffs, New Jersey)

I saw a man sitting on a bench
in Allison Park.
Rain was pouring down,
tears running down his face.
The sky was misty, gray,
fog everywhere enveloping the man,
his world, his town.

Not far away were lovers in a car
not sure they'd meant to go out for a walk,
not then.
Rained in.
They didn't care.

A man was sitting in a maroon Taurus
with the windows halfway down,
reading the paper,
looking at the weather forecast:
Mostly sunny, high of 74.
He chuckles, thinks,
It's pouring down and 63.
So what? It's all the same to me!

The man got up from the bench to go for a walk.
The trail was different—
new trees in the place he used to pray.
Told himself, I should be coming here more often,
but he probably won't.
He's not the pastor anymore.

I saw a man on a bench in Allison Park.
He went for a little walk in the rain, then left.
The sky was misty, gray, just like his life.

Sudden Death

Life changes. Life changes in the instant. You sit
down to dinner and life as you know it ends.
—Joan Didion, The Year
of Magical Thinking

Sudden death:
In sports, it means to lose the game
in overtime, first team to score.
In life, it means to die in a moment,
for evermore.

One moment here, the next one not:
The journey between the two
you never would have thought
could happen.

But it does
in sudden death.

Terminal

Will this pain be my demise?
Am I nearing that final sunrise,
you know, the one we talked about
in a kinda, sorta way?

We'd say,
"If something ever happens
to me someday . . ."
Is it happening?
Is this it?
This pain: I cannot sit
or stand or lie
or go to Europe or the Grand Canyon
or London.

I didn't expect it
to come this way.
Not yet.
Not ever.
Certainly not now.

Beauty That Was

All good things got to come to an end.
The thrills have to fade
before they come 'round again.
—Jackson Browne, "All Good Things"

Chattering chipmunks can be heard
on the well-worn trails
through the woods of Flat Rock Brook.
But sitting near the modest rapids,
the gurgling water
drowns out chipmunk sounds,
cacophonous birds,
and acorns falling to the ground
onto the leaves of autumns past.

The final days of this September
will soon give way
to chilly nights
and swirling, fiery leaves
that now have just a tinge of color.

Chattering Christians at my church
will soon cease to be heard
as our glorious summer
gives way to chilly autumn.
Our season in the sun now segues
down to winter barrenness.

Leaves falling to the ground are tragic,
trees towering naked and exposed,

beauty betrayed as winter solstice cloaks us
in raw, barren darkness.

Strike the shepherd,
and the sheep scatter
like leaves falling to the ground.
I like to watch them flutter
in October,
pay homage to the loveliness that was.

Emphysema

I've got (breath)
emphysema (breath).
My doctor says (breath)(gasp)
it's from smoking (breath).
I'm not so sure (breath).
My Dad had it (breath).
My Mom had it (breath)(gasp).
Could be (breath)
hereditary (breath).
Maybe my lungs (breath)(gasp)
got damaged when (breath)
I had pneumonia (breath)(gasp)
a couple of times (breath).

I still smoke (breath)—
a little (breath)(breath).
But I'm careful (breath)
with the oxygen (breath)
machine (breath).
Smoking (breath)(gasp)
doesn't seem (breath)
to make it (breath)
worse (breath).

My daughter (breath)(gasp)
won't visit (breath)
anymore (breath).
Caught me (breath)
smoking (breath).
Said if I was (breath)

goin' to smoke (breath)
she didn't (breath)
want (breath)
nothing to do (breath)
with me (breath).

I was going (breath)
to move out (breath)
of my (breath)
apart- (breath) (gasp)
ment (breath).
I'm on the (breath)
second floor (breath(gasp).
Can't do the (breath)
stairs (breath).

Every night (breath)
feels like I'm (breath)
dying (breath) (gasp),
suffocating (breath).
I gasp (breath)
for air (breath).

Why did (breath)
God do this (breath)
to me (breath)?
Used to live (breath)
next door (breath)
to a dry cleaners (gasp).
Maybe (breath)
the chemicals (breath)
got me (breath).
I should sue (breath).

But I'm too (breath)(breath)
tired (breath)(gasp)(breath).

Swan Song

This is not how we wanted it to end for him.
Do you remember Willie Mays falling down
in center field the year he played for the Mets
in that 1973 World Series game,
the ball sailing over his head?

Do you remember Elvis
singing during that last year,
stiff and bloated
by fried peanut butter and banana sandwiches
and prescription medications?
No, this was not how we wanted it to end.

We remember golden days
when their greatness gave us pleasure,
but there's no satisfaction in seeing someone's demise.
Do you remember Muhammad Ali
floating like a butterfly
and stinging like a bee
before we saw him slumped
in the corner at Caesar's Palace
after Larry Holmes pummeled him for twelve rounds?

Do you remember Michael Jackson as a young black man
before he started turning more and more pale
until he fell over dead at fifty?

This was certainly not how we wanted it to end.

CPSIA information can be obtained at www.ICGtesting.com
Printed in the USA
BVOW040849230911

271870BV00001B/7/P